THE GOD OF LONGING

BRENT CALDERWOOD

Sibling Rivalry Press
Little Rock, Arkansas
www.siblingrivalrypress.com

Sibling Rivalry Press, LLC
PO Box 26147
Little Rock, AR 72221

info@siblingrivalrypress.com

www.siblingrivalrypress.com

ISBN: 978-1-937420-81-9

Library of Congress Control Number: 2014944842

First Sibling Rivalry Press Edition, September 2014

In memory of two poets,
Phillip Calderwood and Thespyna Christophi

ONE

TWO

THREE

FOUR

one

THE GOLDEN HOUR
for Jérôme

The Hasids and hipsters are out on Prospect Lake.
Little boys, their tzitzis dangling, toss matzo and challah
to monstrous tow-headed swans. They squabble and claw
the soft baked braids while ducks peck holes in the flat crackers,
and the sun bends down to scatter coins on the water.
Each lit ripple has a shadow: itself and the negative of itself.

I want to share my impression
of the orange brownstones,
the cooling sidewalks,
your old black Kodak against my chest,
the way the stretched neck on your T-shirt
shows off your collarbone.
I want to say so much
but instead I lift the camera to my cheek,
its heavy lens propped in my hand like a baby's head,
and I say, "This is the golden hour."
Click, wind, click.

In the next frame,
your mouth is a small o—
you've broken your matinee pose
to look me dead in the eye
and say with languid French vowels,
"You are right, it *is* gold."

Maybe I should tell you
it's just a cliché, but for a moment,
the whole city is silent, burnished.

It will be hours till we're home,
hours before you're translating my poems,
turning the little Germanic nouns
into long Latinate phrases,
and if you ask again what makes them
more than jagged paragraphs,
I still won't have the answer

so for now I stand with you
in simple awe of the salmon-colored sky
waiting for the day to go out like a busted flashbulb.

Nocturne

"Perhaps it is better to wake up after all, even to suffer,
rather than to remain a dupe to illusions all one's life."
— Kate Chopin, *The Awakening*

In dreams, you read my poems, I'm never in bed
past noon, no one snores. I still cook the same
four meals in the Teflon pan. You bake banana bread
drenched in butter, sear pink cubes of tuna, steam
asparagus. A ceramic lamp on your nightstand glows
pink, green, then so smoothly to blue the change
is barely apparent. We drool on the same pillows
for two more years. But aside from my limited range
at the stove, nothing's based in fact. It's fiction,
like the only novel we'd both read, about a flawed
hero who wants more than a well-larded kitchen.
Last night, you wore a hand-lettered sandwich board,
bits of dialogue snatched from the book: *because I*
love you—and on the back, you'd written *Goodbye.*

STAY LITTLE VALENTINE STAY

Each February I raced home from school
and poured the contents onto the floor,
a sort of second Halloween, I ran my hand
over the names of boys   matt dan mike
steve   opened the envelopes they'd licked
shut, dissected each dumb pun, the insect
imploring *Bee Mine*, the stuffed bear

pawing the jar of honey, or robots
made entirely from car parts, flamethrowers
spraying their sparking hearts, ski-masked
turtles named for Renaissance painters
rappelling off the sides of skyscrapers,
all signed in a clumsy scrawl. I thumbed
each punched-out edge, ragged and rough,

shook my box of Sweethearts, crunched
the ones that changed each year: *Groovy,
You Win, You're Rad* and *Fax Me*. I saved
the classics for last: *I Love You, Marry Me,
Say Yes*. The permanent ones. I held them
on my tongue as long as I could, I sucked
the bits of colored chalk till they dissolved.

Ballad of the Kind Young Men

It was different then—
even twenty years ago—
no place for kind young men.

Five, six, eight, ten,
the halls, a shortcut home. I know,
it was different then,

but I can't remember when
I didn't dread that I'd grow
into one of those kind young men

who'd trade a sword for a pen,
the kind slain daily on the radio
in ballads of sad young men—

"Smalltown Boy," "Ben,"
"Ode to Billie Joe"—
because we were different. Then

it happened—what?—when?—
Ellen? AIDS? Margaret Cho?—
A new breed of young men.

In dreams, I'm back in school again.
A softball field. I still can't throw.
It was different then.
Now, they are kind young men.

two

ELEGY

for Phillip Calderwood

At ten a.m. I stole away from your bright white room,
boarded the bus and the train, then exited past black umbrellas,
the big obscene obelisk and naked, rain-soaked cherry trees.
I walked down along the wall of the Vietnam Memorial,
down into the earth, to the year you were born.

When we were seven and nine
we pocketed our latchkeys and marched off to school
with milk money in our shoes,
slow enough to count every BEWARE OF DOG,
every tall kid punching the air,
every newspaper and frost-covered lawn,

so slow that sometimes the bell rang
while we were walking and then—then, brother,
I must have looked at you with something like hate,
for you let out a little wheeze, sat down on the curb,
and I ran and ran till you were a small thing in the distance,
a comma, bent and pausing for breath.

And now look at me: all week I've been walking
as slowly as I can to your bright white room,
the machine breathing for you,
slack bags of red and amber,
tubes going in and taking away.

I walk slowly to the cafeteria,

slowly to the bathroom, slowly to the hotel,

and I walked slowly this morning at eleven a.m.

past fifty-eight thousand, one hundred seventy-eight names,

slowly to the year 1973

and they are too young, all of them.

Brother, this is what I hated:

knowing, even at seven,

that there was no time left,

that I had to go the rest of the way without you.

Two Photographs

1.

The sun shines onto the father's face, he makes a kind of
smile. The house is tiny as a piece of sheet cake. The boys
wear matching khakis and green gingham shirts, they hold
baskets filled with pink plastic grass. The boy on the right has
glasses, he stands in a shadow and clasps his hands like he is
sitting at a desk. The one on the left does not have glasses and
must wear a baseball cap because he likes to cut hair. He has
given himself a tonsure like Friar Tuck, or like the Porky Pig
version of Friar Tuck he has seen on TV. He holds up the back
of his hand like a salute, like he is looking for something far
away. The father has hair like the Beatles on the album *Help!*,
which is packed in a box in the garage. He is holding a baby in
a blue blanket. The baby is crying. He holds it like a plate of
bacon, like a gift he is offering to the camera, a bit of yellow
ribbon curling on top.

2.

It is the same day. The mother stands in front of the house, which squats on the lawn. The sun shines onto the top of her hair, which is brown but she will dye it blond. The baby's head rests between her breasts, its feet press against her diaphragm. The boy with glasses is red. He looks cooked, the way the baby did the day it came home. Both boys have bad hearing. The father picks them up sometimes, he grips them by the side of the head and waves them in the air like bowling trophies. Behind the mother, a door pokes out from the ground. Behind the door is an upright piano. The boy with the baseball cap begs for lessons, but they are expensive and one of the keys is missing. Behind the piano, a metal grille ticks on the floor. It is full of army men and in the winter you can smell them melting. In the winter the piano will be gone.

The camera is big and expensive with many lenses and comes in a real leather case. The mother will have to sell it. The boy in the baseball cap is convinced that if he were bigger he could be trusted with the camera. If he were bigger, he could walk out of the frame and take a picture of the mother, the father, the boy with glasses, and the baby. He would make them look beautiful, he would make them look like a family.

Abecedarius

Already they have decided what he is. He is a
Boy, barely twelve, but to them he is a
Cocksucker, a queer, a sissy.
Denying it only draws attention.
Each day they teach him a new word:
Faggot.
Gay.
Homo.
In the absence of actual proof, these might be idle
Jokes. Maybe the children are just
Kidding when they tell him what his
Lisp means, that he wants to
Marry a boy. He learns
Never to use words that start
Or end with "s."
Plurals are out of the question. Things are singular, or alone. He
Quits going outside at lunchtime. Kids throw
Rocks, scrawl words on his locker,
So he goes to the room marked BOYS at
Twelve each day, pretends to
Urinate, then stays in a stall till the bell rings at one.
Vaguely, he remembers a time before
When he could be here without seeing
X-rated drawings of himself on tiled walls. It was just a

Year ago. He would be here for a minute at the most,
Zip up his pants, then go back outside to play.

Fault Zone

"Since faults usually do not consist of a single, clean fracture,
the term fault zone is used when referring to the zone of complex
deformation that is associated with the fault plane."
      — Tom L. McKnight, *Physical Geography*

1.

Earthquake days, we ducked under our desks
till the rumbling stopped, then went outside to play.
We were taught to cover our necks and faces, the soft parts.
I was soft everywhere, too big to fit under a desk.
Tremors made batches burn
at the Ghirardelli Chocolate Factory in San Leandro.
I can't prove this,
but it's what I remember, the rattle
and the sweet rancor. (Same smell today when I exited Penn Station.
Confection stand near piss-soaked concrete.)

At recess I sat on the same bench as always,
looking through thick lenses
to see where grass in cracked asphalt had been uprooted.
Nothing had moved, it seemed, but later,
on rainy days, coffee cans in skylit hallways
caught water through crazed panes,
the tinny echoes like aftershocks.

I dug holes in the backyard
by the artichoke plant and the apricot tree
searching for arrowheads left by the Ohlones
before the Spanish, Portuguese and Irish settled there.
I found scraps of glass,
beer-bottle brown or cobalt blue, and twice
little ceramic animals,
a fawn and a rabbit from Red Rose Tea packages, and once
a ring. Tourmaline, pink with blue occlusions.

2.

The boys' bodies are unruly.
Mine is all rules. I move it
slowly, wait and watch
each month as the curb pulls
away from the street,
iron grate
       caving in at the
              edge.

Stenciled letters come undone:
       Storm Drain Ru

              ns To Sea

       Please Do No

              t Dump

On TV, Orson Welles is talking about Nostradamus:
He says there will be a major earthquake
in San Francisco in May of 1989.

For the rest of my sixth-grade year,
I keep my toys wrapped in clean
white T-shirts in the closet.
It is the year my mother gives away the old wooden metronome,
the year my father leaves with the piano.

It is the year my godfather dies,
his brown skin pale at the wake.

I begin stuffing a sock in my pants to approximate virility.
I tell no one, but I suspect everyone suspects.

3.

A very slow dance.
　　The quakes beat the time.

Vibrato.
　　Tremolo.
　　　　Wah-wah.
　　Melisma.
Ululation.
Coda.

Jump cut.
　　Verite.
　　Verfremdungseffekt.

Metathesis.
　　Parataxis.
　　　　Chiasmus.
　　　　　　Caesura.
　　　　　Lunfardo.
　　　　Jeringonza.
　　Pig Latin.
Spoonerism.

Frottage.
　　Pressure.
　　　　Climax.
　　Refraction.

Essential tremor.

      Benign tremor.

            Parkinsonian tremor.

      Dystonic tremor.

Cerebellar tremor.

      Psychogenic tremor.

            Orthostatic tremor.

      Physiologic tremor.

4.

First
there is a shock that feels like pain.

The boy runs to the toilet,
releases his fingers. A pearl
slug drops into the bowl.

At school they throw spittle
and a rock to the base of the skull.
There is a shock that feels like pain,
a blurring of vision.

He cannot throw,
so the strong boys make up names
which perfectly illustrate his thoughts.

Nights he pushes the growing thing down.
There is the shock that feels like pain,
a splitting of senses.

Disclosure

I really did cry over spilt milk.
Sobbing at breakfast, napkin in hand,
the broken glass,
the blue skim slick
spread thin as my mother's money.
And when I slipped and skinned my knee, I cried
about the pants, ripped too large for patches.

When even my husky boys' jeans un-
snapped, I tried elastic waistbands.
No loops for the Cub Scout belt
that didn't fit anyway.
Each meeting, the Scouts got to watch
push-ups, my penalty for the incomplete uniform.

When my bike tire got caught in cable car tracks,
I flew forward onto cracked asphalt
and a homeless man asked, *Are you alright?*
—*Yes, I'm fine.*
I walked my mangled bike back home. Gravel
in my legs for two years,
scaly and bumped beneath the surface.
A doctor told me,
When a foreign substance enters the body,
the body expels it or surrounds it in tissue;
it's called invagination.

This is all to say, I have a bad habit of apologizing for accidents.

Ejaculating almost feels that way.

Alone, I'll drowse, then stumble to the shower.

With visitors it is more formal.

I gently clean their bellies with warm facecloths.

Here, I say, wiping quickly, as if the stuff had the power to kill.

Facture

facture   /'fak-chur/ noun
[a. F. *facture*, ad. L. *factura*, f. *facere* to make]
The quality of the execution of a painting;
an artist's characteristic handling of the paint.
—*The Oxford English Dictionary*

The grain of the paper or the weft of the canvas
will affect the visibility of the brushstrokes.
San Francisco was a sheet with a lot of tooth to it,

an ungessoed canvas. Despite my best efforts
at being a *fijnschilder*, fan brushes and feathers
couldn't smooth me out. I had until then

been mannered and minimal more than real.
Vermeer lick finish gave way to Van Gogh impasto,
studio to *en plein air*. Finding the right

medium helped me move between these extremes.
A palette of bruise hues—green gray black
brown blue—became my signature.

three

Catalogue

1. Some of our best inventories of the Roman gods come from Augustine, who mentioned them only to show how arbitrary the old religion was. Abeona, who watches over the child's first steps away from home; Adeona, who brings him back safely. Himeros, god of longing. After school, I would walk to the library to write them down, into the thousands, one for every rock and stream, every stage of gestation and kind of sex, until the children found me there, too.

   The Romans called on four gods to help them remove a particularly stubborn tree—The Pruner, The Breaker-Up, The Burner, and The Carrier-Away.

   * * *

2. In *Psycho*, Janet Leigh lies naked and draped on the bathroom floor, a shower curtain in her hand. It is black and white. She is the color of the curtain. The blood is actually chocolate syrup, which is now made from corn. The swirling drain fades into a close-up of her eye. She must hold the pose, naked and dripping for 40 seconds. We watch with our pause buttons, delighting in the twitch of a lid, the nostril's slight dilation.

   The blood funnels counter-clockwise because of the Coriolis effect. The Lowland Scots called this direction *widdershins*, which means *against the direction of the sun*. But it also sometimes means clockwise. It can mean itself and the opposite of itself, like *dust, sanction,* and *inflammable.*

* * *

3.   The walls are never the problem. It is always the roof that needs replacing. In the whorehouses of Pompeii, ashes have preserved frescoes of the various positions available to customers. There were three female prostitutes to every ten men in Pompeii. They were called *lupae*, wolves.

There are also the crouching mothers and the perfect hands of children. But the thatch roofs burned on impact.

* * *

4.   In the third act of *Vertigo*, Jimmy Stewart gets thrown off Kim Novak's scent. We are expected to believe this. Her hair is de-bleached and un-bunned. She wears a pair of thick, ridiculous eyebrows. In real life Hitchcock wanted to turn her into Grace Kelly, whom he'd lost to the Prince of Monaco. He dyed her hair and taught her to walk like a princess, or a block of ice. He never used her again.

In real life Novak had an affair with Sammy Davis Jr., for which they both received death threats.

* * *

5. Scraps of Sappho lie waiting in perfume jars and caves: bits of stored energy, plant, animal. We are still finding them. A nearly complete poem was found wrapped around the snout of a small embalmed crocodile.

   It might have said, *I am more than your brackets and asterisks, more than the surprise of pronouns.*

   * * *

6. The gooseflesh around your nipples. There is the broken one and the breaker. Sometimes it is that facile.

   There is someone here who looks *just like you*—he's got your eyebrows just right, your pigeon-toed walk. I would use him in my next film, if he were available.

SWIM

Back in our thatched cabin
we washed the sand from our bodies
with a bucket and hose

I could still feel the waves
bucking under me
and the red places

where the brain coral had scratched you
You were growing
like the beach does at dusk

Monkeys braying
in the old Muslim graveyard
something hooting at the moon

and us moving in and out like the tide
The cuts on your legs
shining like stars

INTERMISSION

After the slop and sizzle, I examine your shrinking glans, and, turning it over, the frenulum, the inverted V where your foreskin was once attached. I read somewhere that the removed flesh could cover an index card, though why someone would want to do that I don't know. Now there's a notch in the beveled neck of your arrow, a crease in your paper valentine, a drop stitch in the seam that runs from the equator of your balls down to your perfect ass, which a moment ago held my ring finger. Just shy of the knuckle, I felt a pulse—I didn't know if it was yours or mine.

* * *

less tab and slot
    than convex to concave
belly to small of back
    shoulder pouring itself into a cupped palm

less spuming albumen
    than the fetal sleeper
soft and effeminate
    translucent as a three minute egg

EVOLUTION

1.

It's Winter Solstice in San Francisco, and the Radical Faeries
are throwing a sex party. I have your blessing to go
but instead I bought booties for my brother's new baby,
had your bike tire replaced and came home to write poems.
They're about earthquakes, and you won't believe this, but
this morning there was an earthquake here.
I came from my Harlem apartment to see you,
but you're in Westchester visiting family.
You stopped by Manhattan to get my glasses,
used the keys I made you. I feed your cats.
It's so domestic, I don't know if I can stand it.
But I like your style, the walls you've painted red,
and you even humored me before you left,
went with me to get a Christmas tree.
I've learned to ask for a "Charlie Brown."
The salesman came back with a wonky,
patchy thing, sold it to us for cheap.
It won't stand up straight,
so the little minaret you use for a star leans 45 degrees.
It's fine, I wanted it for the smell anyway.
I cover the water bowl under the tree with aluminum foil
so your cats won't get urinary tract infections.

2.

The mourning doves bill and coo on the bars of your fire escape.
It's almost like having a balcony, and I water
the plants you grow there, but it reminds me
of disaster just the same.
The French call it *roucoulement*—the cooing, I mean.
Ah, their pretty words.
I know a couple who've been together thirty years,
and they've lived that whole time in the same
little studio on Market Street
near the old Mint. Can you imagine?
Some years, pigeons build their nests on the ledge
outside their open shower window.
Well, not nests really.
Pigeons just lay a few twigs
down to keep their eggs from rolling away.
This spring, Ruven decided to put the eggs in a carton and
move them to a lower ledge.
Who knows if the birds abandoned them,
not finding them where they expected,
but it seemed more humane than the previous spring,
when David just flicked them off.

3.

I wrote my first happy song today.
Four major chords.
Does optimism have to be so simple?
The amount of reflection seems so small,
like a convict's mirror.
Maybe I'll put in a minor bridge.
There needs to be an epiphany, doesn't there?
I clipped my toenails,
made a sandwich.

4.

I've eaten too much.
There's a Buddhist idea that this pain
is on equal footing with the pain of
not eating enough.
Pain is pain.
But I wonder if that's an idea put in there
for the American Buddhists.
Like the way the "mother meditation"—
imagining your enemies as your mother,
or imagining them having been your mother in a past life,
I always forget which—
has to be changed to the "grandmother meditation"
for us Westerners.

5.

Does this all sound bourgeois?
I never got to middle-class, I don't know
which parts to detest.
In Amsterdam I came to love the stolid fathers
who walked their daughters to daycare each morning
past the Red Light showrooms—
Armenian hookers in French-cut panties—
without batting an eyelash.
I drank Heinekens with German boys in the punk bar,
watched the flickering video of two women
sewing a third woman's labia together
while a man laid his head on her thigh
and lapped at the blood.
I showered with women at a public pool
with a co-ed locker room. Danced in the gay Muslim bar
on Ramadan, no one drinking,
the women twirling dervishly.
I took my classes in the old hospital
building along the Prinsengracht.
The professor said the connection between sex and love
was just a sociological construct, and a recent one at that.

6.

We talk about the erotic because it is about so much.
You spent the night in your fuckbuddy's bed last week;
the boyfriend (the FB's BF)
tiptoed in the next morning to get his socks from the dresser,
chatted you up casually, then went to work.
Now we discuss whether we can be evolved,
what "evolved" means.

7.

I'll visit Kansas again for work next month, meeting
with those standardized-test specialists.
"Kansas is actually *flatter* than a pancake," one teacher
told me. "They did a study at the university."
The Department of Education puts me up
at the Holiday Inn.
There's a Pac-Man-shaped swimming pool
that all the rooms open onto.
The plants, curtains, sheets, carpet, pillows—
all reek of chlorine, and there's no natural light.
But downtown Lawrence is actually quite charming.
I spot rainbow stickers in cafe windows
and find the gay newspaper and cruisy section
of the KU campus all on the first day.
It feels like going home
because my mother was born in Kansas,
or because I don't feel safe.
The test forms can't mention dinosaurs
because it raises questions about a world
before Jesus, about Darwin.
The phrase "millions of years ago"
gets changed to "a long time ago"
in articles about spiders, planets, or yes, even earthquakes.
When the teachers ask if I'm married, I say "no."

8.

We are becoming family.
Next year we'll spend Christmas together—
things are leaning that way.
The house where the Faeries are having that party is a Victorian,
like all the painted ladies on your block—
they're so easily split:
the servants' quarters become a dungeon,
the madwoman's attic a home office with bay view.
The gingerbread eaves provide shelter for homeless men
who park their shopping carts in the driveway
just long enough to urinate.

9.

I've tried tricking, per our arrangement.
One guy I met in Chelsea,
by the time we got to his brownstone, he said,
"You know your problem? You think too much."
Meditation helps with that, I guess.
And going home with smart people.
Other attempts go better, even well.
I am a dilettante: to connect
without connection is the art.
I think even after we evolve
I'll prefer to stay home with the cats.

10.

At uncertain moments, all the flat states between us
come as a comfort.
After this winter visit, we'll need
some sea change, some shifting fault to move us
      I don't know
            forward, together.
For now, we joke about walking
through wormholes
in a nanosecond
   me to California
      you to New York
then returning to our respective oceans.
Your physicist friend in Berkeley speaks of such things—
wormholes, strings, seven dimensions we don't perceive.
The theories seem silly to me,
the way the archaeopteryx,
Bonobo chimpanzees,
or you or I—you *and* I—
must seem to those teachers,
that professor.
I want to stitch the coasts together
with strong, taut thread.

Song

I tried to write a song about you for my guitar
but it caught somewhere between frets,
stuck in the soundhole, wound in the wire
and wood and wouldn't sound out. I guess
this is how the ancients felt when they tried
to describe how Order came from Chaos.
They knew all about the chasm, the void,
the gap, the demiurgical tear, but were at a loss
to explain how anything good came out
of it. I understand now why Plato and the rest
argued for hours on their little couches about
the origins of Love. We are hatched in the nest
of Chaos. We know lack, strife; Eros
is just a toddler with license to bear arrows.

GOAT ROCK

Hours ago, we walked as far west as walking would take us,
faltered over basalt, soaking my sandals, your boots,
to stare at starfish—some withering on crags,
others shoving whatever into their white mouth-bodies.
We studied tide pools where Russian River meets Pacific,
troubled anemones with one finger,
watched dime-sized crabs scuttle under algae,
then scudded uphill over gravel and sand,
silk-soft shards of glass, driftwood eels,
kelp held high like balloons.

Now on this ridge, it looks like six inches
from rising tide to the road that drove us here.
If we were cartographers, we could sketch the coastline
for miles. Instead we take pictures to share.
I like climbing to the top where salt air
stings my nostrils, but today I wait
in lupine and Queen Anne's lace,
and while you scale the highest bit
I find a patch of iceplants to rest on.
I want to impress you with the names of wildflowers,
but when you return you kneel into me, turn,
and I hold you, tall as me, in my arms.

Next summer, we'll return on separate trips.
On another beach, I'll spy your new tattoo—
raw anemone troubled by other hands,
red sun setting under thick rope of neck,
your beautiful naked body no longer naked.

But on this ridge, wind whips fog on our soft pink faces
and I smell the thin wisp of your hairline.
I'm holding you, *like a baby*, I'm thinking.
I'm thinking, *It doesn't get any better.*

Corpse Plant

Your last visit, we drank our fair trade blend,
then took the train to Brooklyn to see the thing
famed for the smell of rotting mammals.

*Amorphophallus titanium: Imported from Sumatra, grows
seven to ten feet once a decade. Produces a single bloom
which begins wilting after twelve hours.*

Today, a photo I didn't know you'd taken—
the back of my head, first hint of thinning,
and the flower, its huge putrid stamen already gone.

DOG VILLANELLE

Human beings are so complex.
Dogs are easier to understand.
They do whatever one expects.

Dogs don't conflate love with sex.
They listen to your reprimands,
but human beings are so complex.

Nor do dogs order brand-new checks
with two names and an ampersand.
They do whatever one expects.

I saw you at the Cineplex
with someone new—you two held hands.
Human beings are so complex.

I wonder if he ever reflects
on why you make so many demands—
or, do you do whatever he expects?

In my novel, I'll call you Rex—
a dog's name more than a man's.
Human beings are so complex.
They do whatever one expects.

Man Friday

I'm alone on this island—you're gone—there's nothing to do.
I'm walking down Bleecker—last week I was walking with you.
I don't know a soul in this whole goddamn city of light.
Goodbye Man Friday, hello Saturday night.

I need a distraction, a break from this prison of blue.
I'm a fellow on furlough who fell in the first round for you.
You threw in the towel while I stood in the ring for the fight.
Goodbye Man Friday, hello Saturday night.

Someday we'll be friends, then you'll probably answer my calls.
We'll have monthly dinners and talk about nothing at all.
Till then I will scour the bars with my heart locked up tight.
Goodbye Man Friday, hello Saturday night.

Thaw

Central Park, New York

The Harlem Meer is thawing.
Swans shove their ridiculous necks into the muck,
fathers and sons hold their poles over the rim,
straight and slouching.
A sign reads "Catch & Release Only."
Geese that pecked pith from reeds all winter
graze like fat brown cows on lawns,
snow huddles in brindled chunks on pathways,
grackles chirr their throaty hosannas.
First blossoms look like frost that won't go,
or like the salt in your hair.

If you were here, you'd hear the train mole under us,
you'd see the lake shake at intervals—
predictable, so different from the fault back home.
If you stayed long enough, you'd see the line jerk tight,
the grinding reel, and the dripping fish,
gray as the lake, belly white as sky.
You'd see scales fall like subway tiles,
see the body flutter and go limp, surrender to thumbs.
"Yes, let go. Let go," you'd say
if you were here.

It floats when it's thrown back,
belly half-turned to sky,
then skitters off,
a glimmer in the gloom.

We Return Our Squandered Bodies to Their Separate Rooms

The day came on ordinary as yellow mustard. The air tasted like metal. My thumbs were numb from texting. You looked as bad as I felt, you looked like a migraine. We were listening to Joni Mitchell at Cafe Flore. No, it was Fleetwood Mac, and you looked so good you made my teeth sweat. We fell through the sidewalk and came out the other side where we ordered clinking drinks from emperor penguins with trays on their flippers, or should I say wings. You always knew how to pass the lunch hour. "The marbleized water isn't safe to drink," you said, "it's full of bits of plastic." "They say tears of joy are a myth," I said, "we're really just releasing grief." "Who's they," my mother used to say. We were just ourselves that summer, useless as cummerbunds, when we drove past miles of warm bread fields.

Rain

Here comes the rain again.
The tsunami came to Japan yesterday
and five thousand miles to the east
the bay is huge, swaying and gray,
an elephant butting its head into the dunes.
When the plovers come back tomorrow,
they'll perforate the sand in neat little rows,
searching for whatever it is plovers eat.

I want to walk in the open wind.
But it's coming so hard I have to hold
my umbrella like a riot shield,
the metal legs straining in the squall.
I should pick up a phone. I should call
my sister-in-law. She lost her husband on Friday.
I should call my mother, who lost one of her sons
but who does that anymore—pick up a phone, I mean?
We carry them with us.

I want to talk like lovers do.
The night of the election
I was missing your big kitchen,
the seasoned pan, that trick you taught me
for cutting onions. The next morning
it was like the poster said, HOPE—

I even thought of calling you,
even forgot about the marriage amendment.
My family didn't—think to call, I mean.
No one said, "It's not fair."

I want to dive into your ocean.
In the video, Annie Lennox
is walking into the sea like Virginia Woolf,
or, if that was a river, then like James Mason
at the end of *A Star Is Born*.
MTV wouldn't play her at first—
Annie Lennox, I mean.
They said she looked too much like a man.

Is it raining with you?
Last week I saw a seal pup wash onto the shore,
a black purse spilling open with opals, rubies,
so fresh the gulls hadn't found it yet—
they were still squawking downwind
round a crab, and when I came close they flew off.
Their feet had scratched out a wreath of little V's,
three rows deep, each pointing out from the middle,
away from the ticking thing,
half-eaten, half-alive.

The Way We Walk

Now we walk the way
we argued:
in circles.
We keep running into each other.

Like we argued
(often),
we keep running into each other.
Maybe you think I'm stalking you.

Often
I'm ashamed when we meet.
It feels like I'm stalking you,
gun in my pocket.

I'm ashamed when we meet.
My need hangs like a
gun in my pocket,
no safety on.

My need hangs like a
fish—
no safety on
the end of a line.

I fish—
have we come to
the end of the line?
How funny.

We've come to.
We're indifferent.
Funny how
we used to come together.

We're in different
circles.
We used to come together.
Now we walk away.

four

GRETEL REMEMBERS

To hear the experts tell it,
you open a boy's head and there's a silicon grid in there,
a cork bobbing on water, the needle always pointing north.
And mine's a small walnut,
plumping each day with clipped recipes,
last lines from novels and a million shrieking soliloquies.

But who was it who refused to bring a map,
who made a trail of breadcrumbs for the birds to eat?
And when his fingers turned to Vienna sausages,
when the pinch test came—who whittled a stick
for her brother to poke through the iron bars?
The blind bat wanted him soft as foie gras.
By the ninth week he'd grown cheeks
like baked apples, his boy breasts ripe with white meat.

For five months, I was kept on a diet
of beet roots and lamb's lettuce.
I watched moss grow on the north side of the nutmeg trees
and charted the stars through small panes of barley sugar
while the hag slept.

I slaved away at the oven,
dutifully scraping suet into serving bowls,
punching huge yeasty mounds of pumpernickel

and tossing them like medicine balls into larded pans.
I grunted daily over the churn till my soft arms hardened,
I pulled great strands of taffy till the muscles on my back
splayed into a pair of strong wings.
When the feast day came, there'd be no do-overs,
no extra innings. I had one shot.

At first, the reporters had a field day:
"Local Senior Barbecued by Juvenile Delinquents"
and then "Missing Stepmother Forced Husband
to Abandon Children, Father Acquitted."

Things gradually went back to normal,
though Hansel seems a bit depressed.
He sits on the couch all day, smelling faintly of veal.
From the kitchen, I can hear the sports scores,
the latest news, and those stories about
how our brains make us different.
I even recognize some of their voices:
They never commented on my brother's weight,
they never asked me how I knew the way home.

In the Hall of Primitive Mammals

"Then God told Adam to name the animals…
Yet as he named them, he set himself apart. And
the first animal he named was the unicorn."

The rains came. You alone stayed behind,
bearded and obsessed with your reflection.
For years I clutched books to my rib cage
while the children gathered. On torn pages,
tapestries showed you lion-tailed, goat-hoofed,
human-eyed, drowning in the Flood, hunted
to extinction for your beautiful, fluted horn.
Now, down the hall from the mastodon,
someone's stuck a tusk on a stuffed horse,
set it next to Barnum's mermaid, her torso
rotting under glass. Placards say you're a scribe's
typo, a rhino or ibex seen sideways. Lively
theories, nothing more. The children laugh,
pointing at what their small hands can't grasp.

Leda in Prospect Park

It's two a.m.
This lake swells
with twin possibilities.

On one bank, the sudden thrust
of godhead. Flutter, flap, then gone.

On the other, the slink
and spring of mortal coil,
fumble of sheepskin and gold coin.

My pockets bulge
with breadcrumbs.

Echo

"Narcissus ran from her, calling, 'I'd sooner die
Than let you throw your chains around me.'
'Chains around me,' Echo replied."

Our bed was a lake
he held himself over

crying *I love you*
until his arms gave out

Me underneath
mouthing the words

AUBADES

are never
delivered
at dusk.

We need the night
to kiss lovers
goodbye

part by part, then
come

morning,
depart.

Anal Bleaching Is All the Rage

"Anal bleaching is all the rage."
So says the latest magazine.
How dearly the world loves a cage.

The model's body's bald and beige—
his bottom's got a glossy sheen.
Anal bleaching is all the rage.

They're selling stuff on every page,
but really—anal bleaching cream?
How dearly the world loves a cage.

Will a pinker sphincter truly assuage
your dread that you'll end up a lonely queen?
Is anal bleaching all the rage?

Grand passions get acted out on the world stage.
It's clear, even on your TV screen,
how dearly the world loves a cage.

But, don't fret about raising the minimum wage
or bringing our troops home—just primp and preen.
Anal bleaching is all the rage.
How dearly the world loves a cage.

Soporific

Nights when I'd been tucked in
and all the sheep were counted
I taught myself to drift off
by moving through the dictionary
pairing every letter
with every other letter,
A for aardvark, able, actor
and adding machine
all the way to azure or hazmat,
then bat, rabbit with its two B's
sticking up like ears, and hubcap,
rubdown and so on to subzero
so that I'd pass out by the time
I reached D.
But tonight without you
to tucker me out, I went well beyond
the M and N of insomnia,
O of boredom and loss,
and through the hardest part:
Xanax, ex-boyfriend, multiple X's
of moonshine and porn,
but only by cheating—names,
abbreviations, clumsy hyphens—
it took all the tricks I knew
to get to the end, where the Z's
were lined up, waiting.

Headless Men

> *"We didn't need dialogue. We had faces. There just aren't*
> *any faces like that anymore."*
> — Silent-film star Norma Desmond, *Sunset Boulevard*

"We had faces."
A line from a movie no one sees.
They are all headless men.

We used to read books in a leather den,
then head to the tearoom on our knees.
We had faces.

Now we're online till god-knows-when
for a knight with a horse in his BVDs,
but they are all headless men,

either chopped at the neck like a free-range hen
or cropped at the crotch like limbless trees.
We had faces;

then we found gyms—and amen!—
we could be beautiful, built to please.
Perfect, headless men.

I wish we'd take to the streets again
and fight for love or against disease.
We had faces.
Now we're headless men.

THE GOD OF LONGING

notes

"Stay Little Valentine Stay": The title is taken from the song "My Funny Valentine," lyrics by Lorenz Hart, 1937.

"Rain": The italicized lines are taken from the Eurythmics song "Here Comes the Rain Again," lyrics by Annie Lennox and David A. Stewart, 1984.

"In the Hall of Primitive Mammals": The epigraph is taken from the book *The Unicorn* by Nancy Hathaway (Random House, 1987); the passage is a traditional Western folk variation of Genesis 2:20, in which Adam names the animals. The Hall of Primitive Mammals is in the Museum of Natural History in New York City.

"Echo": The epigraph is taken from Book III of Ovid's *Metamorphoses*, author's translation.

acknowledgments

Grateful acknowledgment is made to the editors of the publications in which the following poems first appeared:

A&U: "Ballad of the Kind Young Men," "Disclosure"
American Poetry Journal: "Song"
Black Robert Journal: "Evolution"
Bloom: "Headless Men"
Caesura: "Elegy"
Crab Creek Review: "Gretel Remembers"
The Gay & Lesbian Review Worldwide: "Anal Bleaching Is All the Rage"
Gertrude: "Abecedarius"
GuyWriters: "Man Friday"
The Innisfree Poetry Journal: "Facture"
Knockout: "In the Hall of Primitive Mammals"
Locuspoint: "Nocturne"
Poets & Artists: "Fault Zone," "Stay Little Valentine Stay," "Two Photographs," "We Return Our Squandered Bodies to Their Separate Rooms"
Slow Trains: "Aubades," "The Way We Walk"
The Squaw Valley Review: "Catalogue"

"The Golden Hour" was selected by Mark Doty as winner of the Atlanta Queer Literary Festival Broadside Contest, 2011.

"Goat Rock" and "Thaw" were published in the anthology *Poets Eleven* (San Francisco Public Library, 2010).

"Nocturne" and "Rain" were published in *The Southern Poetry Anthology* (Texas A&M University Press, 2012).

"Intermission" was published in *The Body Electric* (Ars Omnia, 2013).

"Disclosure" was published in the anthology *Art & Understanding: Literature from the First Twenty Years of A&U* (Black Lawrence Press, 2014).

I wish to express my thanks to the following writers and teachers for their advice and encouragement: Rabih Alameddine, Dorothy Allison, Mark Doty, Robert Hass, Eloise Klein Healy, Brenda Hillman, Cathy Park Hong, Major Jackson, Wayne Koestenbaum, Jaime Manrique, Michael Nava, Sharon Olds, and D. A. Powell.

Very special thanks to Ricardo Avila, Bill Blackburn, William Bonnell, Leslie Canaan, David O'Steinberg, Diane Parker, and Walter Rieman; and, finally, to Bryan Borland and Seth Pennington for the great care they put into the editing and publishing process.

about the poet

Brent Calderwood is a writer and editor living in San Francisco.
His poems have appeared in *American Poetry Journal, Bloom, Crab
Creek Review, Knockout, The Gay & Lesbian Review Worldwide, The
Squaw Valley Review*, and *The Southern Poetry Anthology*. His essays
have appeared in the *Chicago Sun-Times*, the *San Francisco Examiner*,
OUT Magazine, and *Gathered Light: The Poetry of Joni Mitchell's
Songs*. He has received awards and fellowships from the Lambda
Literary Foundation, the San Francisco Public Library, the Napa
Valley Writers Conference, and the Squaw Valley Community of
Writers. He is Literary Editor for *A&U Magazine*.

www.brentcalderwood.com

about the press

Sibling Rivalry Press is an independent publishing house
based in Little Rock, Arkansas. Our mission is to publish
work that disturbs and enraptures.

www.siblingrivalrypress.com

CPSIA information can be obtained
at www.ICGtesting.com
Printed in the USA
FFOW04n1756230115
10476FF